ALL ABOUT ABORTION AND ABORTION LAW IN THE US

Daniel Fitch

All rights reserved. No part of this book may be reproduced or used in any manner without the written permission of the copyright owner except for the use of quotations in a book review.

Book design by Tyson James

ISBN 913-1-8966-4660-9 (ebook)

Copyright Daniel Fitch, 2022

Table of Contents

[Chapter 1](#)

[Chapter 2](#)

[Chapter 3](#)

[Chapter 4](#)

[Chapter 5](#)

[Chapter 6](#)

INTRODUCTION

The legitimateness of Abortion law in the United States is dependent upon individual state regulations. In 1973, Roe v. Swim made the primary early termination case to be taken to the Supreme Court, which had made it governmentally legitimate. In 1992, Roe was to some extent upset by Planned Parenthood v. Casey, which expressed that states can't put lawful limitations representing an unjustifiable weight for "the reason or impact of setting a significant hindrance in the way of a lady looking for an early termination of a nonviable fetus." In 2022, both Roe and Casey were upset by Dobbs v. Jackson Women's Health Organization, and fetus removals (abortions) are presently dependent upon guidelines in light of state regulations once again. Individual states can manage and restrict the utilization of early termination, some of which as of now have used "trigger regulations", which made early termination unlawful inside the first and second trimesters when Roe was overturned.

Chapter 1

CURRENT LEGAL STATUS ACROSS THE COUNTRY

Under the ongoing legal translation of the U.S. Constitution, states have wide circumspection to disallow or manage fetus removal. In Dobbs v. Jackson (2022), the Supreme Court of the United States switched its milestone administering safeguarding fetus removal in Roe v. Swim (1973) and resulting choices that held that fetus removal should be legitimate for a very remarkable pregnancy however might be limited by the states to changing degrees. States have passed regulations to confine late-term fetus removals, require parental warning for minors, and order the divulgence of early termination risk data to patients preceding the method. As of now, governing bodies in 22 states state they would move to boycott or further limit early termination regulations all through the U.S.

The critical pondered article of the US Constitution is the Fourteenth Amendment, which expresses that:

All people conceived or naturalized in the United States, and dependent upon the purview thereof, are residents of the United States and the State wherein they dwell. No State will make or authorize any regulation which will abbreviate the honors or susceptibilities of residents of the United States; nor will any State deny any individual of life, freedom, or property, without fair treatment of regulation; nor deny to any individual inside its purview the equivalent assurance of the laws.

The authority report of the US Senate Judiciary Committee given in 1983 after broad hearings on the Human Life Amendment (proposed by Senators Orrin Hatch and Thomas Eagleton), expressed:

In this way, the [Judiciary] Committee sees that no huge lawful hindrances of any sort at all exist today in the United States for a lady to get a fetus removal under any condition during any phase of her pregnancy.

One part of the legitimate early termination system presently set up has been deciding when the hatchling is "suitable" outside the belly as a proportion of when the "life" of the baby is its own (and subsequently likely to be safeguarded by the state). In the larger part assessment conveyed by the court in Roe v. Swim, suitability was characterized as "possibly ready to live external the lady's belly, yet with a counterfeit guide. Practicality is typically positioned at around seven months (28 weeks, approx. 196 days) however may happen prior, even at 24 weeks." When the court controlled in 1973, the then-current clinical innovation proposed that suitability could happen as soon as 24 weeks. Progresses throughout recent many years have permitted babies that are half a month under 24 weeks old to make due external the belly. These logical accomplishments, while life-putting something aside for untimely children have made the assurance of what is "practical" to some degree more convoluted. The most youthful kid remembered to have endured an untimely birth in the United States was Amillia Taylor (brought into the world on October 24, 2006, in Miami, Florida, at 21 weeks and 6 days gestational age, approx. 153 days versus potentially anticipated gestational time of 40 weeks, approx. 280 days).

Contrasted with other created nations, the methodology is more accessible in the United States as far as how late the early termination can lawfully be performed. Be that as it may, as far as different angles, for example, government subsidizing, protection for non-grown-ups, or topographical access, a few US states are undeniably more prohibitive. In most European nations early termination on request is permitted exclusively during the principal trimester, with fetus removals during later phases of pregnancy permitted exclusively for explicit reasons (for example physical or psychological wellness reasons, the chance of birth abandons, assuming that the lady was assaulted and so on.). The reasons that can be summoned by a lady looking for early termination after the main trimester differs by country, for example, a few nations, like Denmark, give a large number of reasons, including social and monetary ones.

There are no regulations or limitations directing fetus removal in Canada, while the law on early termination in Australia shifts by state/area. In numerous nations, fetus removal has been sanctioned by particular parliaments, while in the US early termination has been considered an established right by the Supreme Court.

In light of the split between the government and state regulation, legitimate admittance to early termination keeps on differing to some degree by state. Geographic accessibility, be that as it may, differs decisively, with 87% of US regions having no fetus removal provider. Moreover, because of the Hyde Amendment, many state wellbeing programs which unfortunate ladies depend on for their medical care don't cover early terminations; presently just 17 states (counting California, Illinois, and New York) offer or require such coverage.

The 1992 instance of Planned Parenthood v. Casey upset Roe's severe trimester recipe, yet reemphasized the right to early termination as grounded in the general feeling of freedom and security safeguarded under the Due Process Clause of the Fourteenth Amendment to the United States Constitution: "On the off chance that the right of protection makes a difference, it is the right of the individual, wedded or single, to be liberated from ridiculous legislative interruption into issues so essentially influencing an individual as the choice whether to bear or bring forth a kid." Advancements in clinical innovation implied that a hatchling may be viewed as feasible, and hence have a premise of a right to life, at 22 or 23 weeks as opposed to at 28 which was more normal at the time Roe was chosen. Hence, the old trimester recipe was managed out of date, with another attention to the suitability of the hatchling.

Beginning around 1995, driven by Congressional Republicans, the US House of Representatives and US Senate have moved a few times to elapse measures forbidding the methodology of flawless widening and extraction, likewise generally known as incomplete birth fetus removal. After a few long and profound discussions on the issue, such measures were passed two times by significant spaces, however, President Bill Clinton rejected those bills in April 1996 and October 1997 separately, because they did exclude wellbeing exemptions. Legislative allies of the bill contended that a wellbeing exemption would deliver the bill unenforceable, since the Doe v. Bolton choice characterized "wellbeing" in obscure terms, legitimizing any thought process in acquiring an early termination. Resulting in Congressional efforts to supersede the rejection being fruitless.

On October 2, 2003, with a vote of 281-142, the House again endorsed an action restricting the methodology, called the Partial-Birth Abortion Ban Act. Through this regulation, a specialist could have to deal with upwards of two years in jail and face common claims for performing such early termination. A lady who goes through the method can't be indicted under the act. The action contains an exception to permit the strategy assuming the lady's life is compromised.

On October 21, 2003, the United States Senate passed a similar bill by a vote of 64-34, with various Democrats participating in help. The bill was endorsed by President George W. Bramble on November 5, 2003, however, a government judge obstructed its implementation in a few states only a couple of hours after it became public regulation. The Supreme Court maintained the cross-country restriction on the technique for the situation Gonzales v. Carhart on April 18, 2007. The 5-4 decision said the Partial-Birth Abortion Ban Act doesn't struggle with past Court choices in regards to fetus removal.

The choice was denoted whenever the court first permitted a prohibition on an early termination starting around 1973. The swing vote, which came from moderate equity Anthony Kennedy, was joined by Justices Antonin Scalia, Clarence Thomas, and the two ongoing deputies, Samuel Alito and Chief Justice John Roberts.

Chapter 2

STATE ADMINISTRATIVE DRIVES IN REGARDS TO ABORTION

States with trigger regulations or pre-Roe prohibitions on early termination that would make fetus removal unlawful in the state if Roe v. Swim were toppled
  Trigger regulations set up
  Trigger regulations and pre-Roe regulations set up
  Pre-Roe regulations set up
The accompanying states have or had driven in regards to fetus removal. The fetal heartbeat bill administrative methodology got energy in 2018 and 2019.

Alabama
Principal article: Abortion in Alabama
Following the Supreme Court overruling of Roe v. Swim on June 24, 2022, early termination is unlawful in Alabama.

A pre-Roe early termination boycott, last corrected in 1951, stays on the books. The law boycotts fetus removals in all cases but to save the existence of the mother. Those sentenced under the rule would confront a most excellent fine of $1,000 and a most extreme prison season of a year.

Playing out an early termination is a Class A lawful offense with as long as 99 years in jail, and endeavored fetus removal is a Class C crime deserving of 1 to 10 years in jail, under a forthcoming regulation passed in May 2019. The law was ordered, however since Roe has been toppled, the law could go into effect.

Early termination is a disruptive issue in the state, with 37% of grown-ups accepting it ought to be legitimate in the whole or most cases and 58% accepted it ought to be unlawful in the whole or most cases. Alabama's political and general strict convictions have given Alabama inhabitants restricted admittance to fetus removal administrations. Starting around 2021, just three centers stay in Alabama, which are all situated in the metropolitan region of the state.

Gold country

Fundamental article: Abortion in Alaska

Up to an authorized doctor carrying out the methodology, early termination is lawful in Alaska. Individuals younger than 17 absolute requirements parental consent.

In 2019, House Bill 178 was proposed, which would have prohibited early termination with no exceptions. The Bill was withdrawn.

Arizona

Primary article: Abortion in Arizona

Fetus removal is lawful as long as 24 weeks of pregnancy. Patients should meet with a doctor no less than 24 hours before the method, and an authorized doctor should carry out the technique. Minors should get parental consent.

Arkansas

Principal article: Abortion in Arkansas

After the Supreme Court upset Roe v. Swim on June 24, 2022, a 2021 trigger regulation produced results in Arkansas that prohibited abortions. The boycott has an exemption for early terminations performed to save the existence of the mother, however, it is conceivable a special case will be made in assault and inbreeding cases in the still up in the air to have played out a fetus removal have to deal with upwards of 10 years in jail and fines up to $100,000.

California

Fundamental article: Abortion in California

Early termination is legitimate in California. Nurture maternity specialists and other non-doctor clinical faculty with appropriate preparation might carry out the methodology. State-funded colleges are legally necessary to give Mifepristone at no expense to students.

Colorado

Principal articles: Colorado Amendment 48 (2008) and Abortion in Colorado

Early termination is lawful in Colorado. Minors' folks or legitimate gatekeepers should get notice before the procedure.

In 2008, Kristine and Michael Burton of Colorado for Equal Rights proposed Colorado Amendment 48, a drive to change the meaning of an individual to "any person from the snapshot of fertilization." On November 4, 2008, the drive was turned near 73.2 percent of the voters.

The state passed the Reproductive Health Equity Act into regulation in April 2022, which safeguards early termination freedoms and guarantees that "each individual has a central right to come to conclusions about the person's regenerative medical services, including the basic right to utilize or reject contraception; a pregnant individual has a major right to proceed with a pregnancy and conceive an offspring or to have an early termination and to settle on conclusions about how to practice that right; and a prepared egg, incipient organism, or baby doesn't have autonomous or subsidiary privileges under the laws of the state."

Connecticut

Primary article: Abortion in Connecticut

The 1821 fetus removal law of Connecticut is the principal realized regulation passed in America to confine early termination.

Albeit this regulation didn't totally ban early terminations, it set heavier limitations as it kept ladies from endeavoring or getting fetus removals, which was for the most part through the utilization of toxins, during the initial four months of a lady's pregnancy.

Delaware

Fundamental article: Abortion in Delaware

Early termination in Delaware is lawful. 55% of grown-ups said in a survey by the Pew Research Center that early termination ought to be lawful on the whole or in most cases. There were restorative special cases in the state's regulative prohibition on early terminations by 1900. Informed assent regulations were on the books by 2007. As of May 14, 2019, the state precluded early terminations after the baby was suitable, for the most part, a few points between weeks 24 and 28. This period involves a standard characterized by the US Supreme Court in 1973 with the Roe v. Swim administering.

Florida

Primary article: Abortion in Florida

Early termination in Florida is lawful up to the 24th seven-day stretch of pregnancy. 56% of grown-ups said in a survey by the Pew Research Center that early termination ought to be legitimate on the whole or in most cases. An early termination boycott with a helpful exemption was set up by 1900. Such regulations were set up after the American Medical Association tried to condemn early termination in 1857. By 2007, the state had a standard informed assent arrangement for fetus removals. By 2013, state Targeted Regulation of Abortion Providers (TRAP) regulation applied to drug actuated early terminations. Endeavors to boycott fetus removal occurred in 2011, 2012, 2013, 2014, 2015, and 2016. Two fetal heartbeat bills were documented in the Florida Legislature in 2019.

Georgia

Primary article: Abortion in Georgia (U.S. state)

Georgia passed a fetus removal regulation on May 7, 2019, which disallows early terminations after a fetal heartbeat is distinguished, typically a month and a half following the last feminine period. The law makes no exemption for instances of assault or incest. The legality of the law was tested by the American Civil Liberties Union, Planned Parenthood, and the Center for Reproductive Rights. In October 2019, the government judge managing the case impeded the implementation of the boycott, which was to produce results in January 2020, expressing that the offended parties have shown a probability of winning the case.

Hawaii

Principal article: Abortion in Hawaii

Starting around 2017, 28 centers in Hawaii will perform early terminations. As of January 2021, early termination can be performed after suitability on the off chance that the patient's life or by and large wellbeing is in danger.

Idaho

Principal article: Abortion in Idaho

Early termination is supposed to be lawful until thirty days following the overruling of Roe v. Swim on June 24, 2022. After the trigger regulation comes full circle, specialists who perform fetus removals will serve something like two years in jail, and up to five years. Exceptions to the boycott will incorporate saving the existence of the mother, as well as legal proof that the pregnancy is the consequence of assault or incest.

Some state chiefs, including Lt. Gov. Janice McEachin "are calling for much stricter regulations, including taking out the special cases for assault, interbreeding, and the existence of the mother and pushing to order early termination as crime murder."

Illinois

Fundamental article: Abortion in Illinois

Early termination is legitimate in Illinois for as long as 24 weeks. Parental assent isn't needed for minors, but a watchman beyond 21 years old should be told except if overturned by an adjudicator in unique cases. Illinois has 40 offices that can perform early terminations as of 2017.

Indiana

Primary article: Abortion in Indiana

Fetus removal is legitimate as long as 22 weeks in Indiana. New 2021 regulations set up in the state require an ultrasound to be finished and displayed to the patient 18 or more hours before the method as well as state commanded directing for the patient. If the patient looking for a fetus removal is a minor, they should get parental assent before moving forward.

Iowa

Primary article: Abortion in Iowa

Fetus removal is lawful in Iowa as long as six weeks following a singular's last period, with special cases relating to the mother's health.

On March 26, 2020, Governor Kim Reynolds developed past COVID-19 calamity announcements to stop elective and trivial surgeries. The next day her office stated: "[The] Proclamation suspends all unimportant or elective medical procedures and techniques until April sixteenth, that incorporates careful fetus removal procedures".

Kansas

Fundamental article: Abortion in Kansas

Kansas administrators supported clearing hostile to fetus removal regulation (HB 2253) on April 6, 2013, which says life starts at treatment, restricts early termination in light of orientation, and restrictions Planned Parenthood from giving sex training in schools.

In 2015 Kansas turned into the principal state to boycott the widening and clearing technique, a typical second-trimester fetus removal procedure. But the new regulation was subsequently struck somewhere near the Kansas Court of Appeals in January 2016 while never having gone into effect. In April 2019, the Kansas Supreme Court confirmed the lower court's choice and decided that the right to early termination is intrinsic inside the state's constitution and bill of freedoms, to such an extent that regardless of whether Roe v. Swim is upset and the government security of early termination privileges is removed, the right would, in any case, be permitted inside Kansas, excepting an adjustment of the state constitution. After the two Houses of the Kansas State Legislature passed an established correction to upset the Kansas Supreme Court's decision, Kansas electors will choose whether to upset the Kansas Constitution on the right track to early termination in a mandate on August 2, 2022.

Kentucky
Primary article: Abortion in Kentucky
After the Supreme Court toppled Roe v. Swim on June 24, 2022, a 2019 trigger regulation produced results in Kentucky that restricted abortions. The law makes all fetus removals unlawful except for when restoratively required to keep the patient from passing on or getting a "day-to-day existence supporting organ" for all time impaired.

Playing out an early termination is presently a Class C lawful offense, with the detainment of 5 to 10 years and fines of $1,000 to $10,000.

The ACLU declared plans to sue the state in court, guaranteeing that the state constitution perceives early termination as a right. On June 30, 2022, Jefferson County Circuit Judge Mitch Perry gave an impermanent limiting request impending the requirement of the state's fetus removal boycott awaiting additional hearings to decide whether the boycott disregards the Kentucky Constitution. This request briefly permits both elective fetus removal suppliers, which are both situated in Louisville, to briefly continue elective abortions. Both the Kentucky Court of Appeals and the Kentucky Supreme Court rejected a solicitation to break up the controlling order.

Louisiana
Primary article: Abortion in Louisiana

On June 19, 2006, Governor Kathleen Blanco endorsed into regulation a trigger restriction on most types of fetus removal (except if the existence of the mother was in harm's way or her wellbeing would be forever harmed) when it passed the state lawmaking body. Even though she felt avoidance of assault or interbreeding would have "been sensible," she believed she shouldn't reject in light of those reasons. The trigger regulation would possibly come full circle assuming the United States Supreme Court turned around Roe v. Swim. The law would permit the arraignment of any individual who performed or supported a fetus removal. The punishments remember as long as 10 years in jail and a greatest fine of $100,000.

At the point when the Supreme Court toppled Roe v. Swim on June 24, 2022, Louisiana promptly prohibited all fetus removals except those performed to save the mother's life or on account of a fetal anomaly.[20][16] On June 27, in light of a claim by Hope Medical Group for Women and Medical Students for Choice, an adjudicator gave an impermanent controlling request which permitted early terminations to continue in the state.

Before 2022, "Conservatives in the state governing body considered regulation characterizing early termination as a manslaughter," which would imply that ladies who got fetus removals could be accused of murder.

New York
Primary article: Abortion in New York
is known in the U.S. as a regenerative safe-haven state. This implies that fetus removal is lawful and seen as a medical service given by the state. There are roughly 252 offices in New York that perform abortions. In 2019 New York classified fetus removals regulations and security in state regulations. New York State Senator Alessandra Biaggi has proposed a bill that permits the choice for citizens in New York to add to the fetus removal access reserve on their tax documents. This makes more admittance to regenerative medical care in the state.

North Dakota

Primary article: Abortion in North Dakota

After the Supreme Court toppled Roe v. Swim on June 24, 2022, North Dakota moved to boycott "practically all fetus removals except for assault, interbreeding or the where mother's life is at risk." The boycott will require 30 days to go into effect. Performing an early termination will be a Class C felony, deserving as long as five years in jail and up to a $10,000 fine.

Ohio

Primary article: Abortion in Ohio

Ohio has various layers of regulation that makes early termination unlawful, coming about because of different ignored regulations the many years. The rundown underneath goes from generally severe to least.

ORC 2919.198 came full circle in July 2019 which made early termination unlawful after a "fetal heartbeat" can be identified, which is as a rule between five or a month and a half after the principal day of the lady's last feminine period. No special cases are made for assault, inbreeding, or still up in the air to have down condition. Notwithstanding, a special case is made for health-related crises, characterized as a "serious gamble of the significant and irreversible weakness of a significant physical process of the pregnant woman."

Remembered for this regulation is a segment called "invulnerability of pregnant lady," which supersedes punishments for pregnant ladies who embrace an early termination after a "fetal heartbeat" has been detected. This arrival of punishments doesn't stretch out to doctors or specialists who oversee the fetus's removal past a recognizable heartbeat.

As per ORC 2919.17, early termination may not be performed after viability, which, per ORC 2919.16, "signifies the progressive phase of a human baby at which in the assurance of a doctor, given the specific realities of a lady's pregnancy that are known to the doctor and considering clinical innovation and data in all actuality accessible to the doctor, there is a practical chance of the keeping up with and feeding of a daily existence beyond the belly regardless of transitory counterfeit life-supporting support." Viability will, in general, happen in the 24th seven-day stretch of pregnancy.

As per ORC 2919.201, early termination may not be performed if "the plausible post-treatment age of the unborn youngster is twenty weeks or greater." Immunity isn't given in a different segment like ORC 2919.198.

Oklahoma

Fundamental article: Abortion in Oklahoma

In 2016, Oklahoma state officials passed a bill to condemn early termination for suppliers, possibly accusing them off as long as three years in prison. On May 20, 2016, Governor Mary Fallin rejected the bill under the steady gaze of it could become regulation, referring to its phrasing as excessively obscure to endure a legitimate challenge.

Lead representative Kevin Stitt marked three bills in 2021 that presented new limitations on fetus removal. One bill would repudiate a clinical permit for individuals who perform fetus removals, another would boycott early terminations if a heartbeat is identified, and the third would require board-ensured OB-GYN specialists to be the ones in particular who can perform abortions.

Starting around 2022, early termination is right now unlawful generally speaking in Oklahoma. On April 12, 2022, Governor Kevin Stitt endorsed into regulation a bill that prohibited early termination endlessly, except if the existence of the mother was in question, without any exemptions for assault and incest. The punishment for playing out a fetus removal is two to five years imprisonment.

South Dakota

Principal article: Abortion in South Dakota
Principal article: Women's Health and Human Life Protection Act

After the Supreme Court upset Roe v. Swim on June 24, 2022, South Dakota prohibited abortions. The trigger regulation for the boycott had been sanctioned in 2005. Under the new regulation, any individual who prompts a fetus removal is "at legitimate fault for a Class 6 felony," with a limit of two years detainment and $4,000 in fines. An exemption is incorporated to "protect the existence of the pregnant female," given "fitting and sensible clinical judgment."

Tennessee

Principal article: Abortion in Tennessee

In 2019, Tennessee ordered a trigger regulation that would boycott fetus removals 30 days after the overruling of Roe v. Wade. The law incorporates an exemption to save the existence of the not entirely settled to have prompted an early termination could have to carry out 3-15 years in jail, as well as up to $10,000 in fines.

Texas

Fundamental article: Abortion in Texas

The Roe v. Swim case attempted in Texas, remains at the focal point of long periods of public discussion about the issue of abortion. Henry Wade was filling in as District Attorney of Dallas County at that point.

On August 29, 2014, US District Judge Lee Yeakel struck down as illegal two arrangements of Texas' omnibus enemy of fetus removal charge, House Bill 2 which was to become effective on September 1. The guideline would have shut around twelve early termination centers, passing on just eight spots in Texas to get a lawful fetus removal, all situated in significant urban communities. Judge Lee Yeakel decided that the state's guideline was unlawful and would have put an unjustifiable weight on ladies, especially on poor and rustic ladies living in west Texas and the Rio Grande Valley. The legitimate test to the law, at last, arrived at the Supreme Court in Whole Woman's Health v. Hellerstedt (2016) which decided that the law was unlawful, its weight of requiring fetus removal specialists to have confirmation honors at a nearby medical clinic inside 30 miles of the middle to impede a lady's on the whole correct to early termination from Roe v. Swim.

In May 2021, Texas administrators passed the Texas Heartbeat Act, forbidding fetus removals as soon cardiovascular movement can be recognized, normally as soon as about a month and a half into pregnancy, and frequently before ladies realize they are pregnant. To keep away from customary sacred difficulties in light of Roe v. Swim, the law gives that any non-government worker or official, aside from sexual culprits who considered the hatchling, may sue anybody that performs or actuates a fetus removal disregarding the resolution, as well as any individual who "helps or abets the exhibition or incitement of an early termination, including paying for or repaying the expenses of an early termination through protection, etc." The claim might be documented by individuals either regardless of any personal stake. The law contains a special case for fetus removals performed to save the mother's life. The law was tested in courts, however still couldn't seem to have a full conventional hearing as its September 1, 2021, sanctioning date came due. Offended parties looked for a request from the U.S. High Court to prevent the law from happening, yet the Court gave a disavowal of the request late on September 1, 2021, permitting the law to stay essentially. While unsigned, Chief Justice John Roberts and Justice Stephen Breyer composed disagreeing feelings joined by Justices Elena Kagan and Sonia Sotomayor that they would have conceded a directive on the law until a legitimate legal review.

On September 9, 2021, Attorney General Merrick Garland, the United States Department of Justice sued the State of Texas over the Texas Act on the premise that "the law is invalid under the Supremacy Clause and the Fourteenth Amendment, is seized by administrative regulation and disregards the teaching of intergovernmental immunity". Garland additionally noticed that the United States government has "a commitment to guarantee that no state can deny people of their established rights." The Complaint affirms that Texas sanctioned the law "in open resistance of the Constitution". The help mentioned from the U.S. Locale Court in Austin, Texas incorporates a statement that the Texas Act is unlawful, and ordered against state entertainers as well as all confidential people who might bring an SB 8 action. The suit was met with discussion, with pundits referring to worries over the suit's politicized nature and the potential encroachments on nonmilitary personnel rights.

After the Supreme Court upset Roe v. Swim on June 24, 2022, Texas prohibited fetus removals except for when the mother's life is at risk. Completed or endeavored to give of early termination "will be accused of a first-or second-degree crime, and will be dependent upon a common punishment of no less than $100,000" for each abortion. A first-degree lawful offense in Texas is deserving of 5 to 99 years in jail, while a second-degree lawful offense is deserving of 2 to 20 years in jail, with "fines of up to $10,000" being possible.

Utah
Primary article: Abortion in Utah
Following the Supreme Court overruling of Roe v. Swim on June 24, 2022, fetus removal is unlawful in Utah, however, the state incorporates exemptions if the mother's life is in danger, as well as in instances of deadly fetal irregularities, serious mind oddities, assault, or incest. It is a second-degree crime to perform it, deserving of 1 to 15 years in jail and a most extreme conceivable fine of $10,000. On June 27, a Utah judge gave a 14-day limiting request to hinder the implementation of the law.

Virginia
Fundamental article: Abortion in Virginia
Early termination is lawful for as long as 25 weeks. A few restrictions incorporate protection inclusion depending on instances of rape or serious medical issue. Parental assent is likewise expected for minors in Virginia. In 2020, Virginia lead representative, Ralph Northam marked regulations that eliminated a significant number of the limitations on fetus removal that had been set up for quite a long time. Virginia turned into the main state to systematize new securities for early termination in 2020.

Washington
Fundamental article: Abortion in Washington

West Virginia
Fundamental article: Abortion in West Virginia
West Virginia has a pre-Roe early termination boycott, with a special case for safeguarding the existence of the patient, which could become enforceable again.

Wisconsin
Fundamental article: Abortion in Wisconsin
In 2013, Act 37 was passed into regulation, requiring conceding honors for all early termination suppliers inside the state. Conceding honors permits doctors the option to concede a patient to a close-by emergency clinic straightforwardly. The state kept up with this was vital for ladies' wellbeing and security, in any case, general wellbeing authorities and the clinical local area - including the American College of Gynecologists and Obstetricians, Wisconsin Medical Society, and American Public Health Association - go against these prerequisites as pointless and are not grounded in proof-based practice. Not just are these honors hard for early termination doctors to get given the dubious idea of fetus removal, but the Wisconsin regulation required conceding honors to be acquired somewhere around one day of the law's section. After Governor Walker marked the bill into regulation, a government locale court judge in the Western District of Wisconsin right away conceded a primer directive, forestalling its execution. A preliminary was held, and the court forced a super durable directive illegal, with the Judge noticing that the center conclusion was the motivation behind the law as there was just a single day conceded for doctors to get consistence. Further, the decision tracked down that fetus removal inconveniences "are uncommon and are seldom hazardous", subsequently it appears to subvert the contention that this regulation is required for ladies' wellbeing and safety.

The case was pursued by the state's lawyer, at this point, the US Seventh Circuit Court of Appeals maintained the prior administering and the extremely durable order. The requests court proclaimed, as did the preliminary court judge, that the state had neglected to exhibit any undeniable requirement for this legislation. The state additionally engaged the Supreme Court, notwithstanding, this allure was dismissed, keeping up with the long-lasting order of the law. The dismissal by the Supreme Court to hear the case came rather rapidly after the decision in the province of Texas' case additionally including conceding honors. The Supreme Court's decision in Whole Women's Health v. Hellerstedt found that the conceding honors prerequisite made an unnecessary weight for ladies, and consequently obstructed the privileges laid out in Roe v. Swim.

Wyoming
Primary article: Abortion in Wyoming
Wyoming has a trigger regulation, which will produce results upon confirmation by the Governor, who is exhorted by the Attorney General by July 24, 2022 (in 30 days of the Supreme Court ruling). Performing a fetus removal will be deserving of as long as 14 years in prison.

Chapter 3

In Response to the Covid pandemic

Primary article: Impact of the COVID-19 pandemic on early termination in the United States

In the midst of the COVID-19 pandemic, hostile to fetus removal government authorities in a few American states established or endeavored to sanction limitations on early termination, describing it as an unimportant strategy that can be suspended during the clinical emergency. The orders have prompted a few lawful difficulties and analysis by common freedoms gatherings and a few public clinical associations, including the American Medical Association. Legal difficulties for fetus removal suppliers, large numbers of which were addressed by the American Civil Liberties Union and Planned Parenthood, effectively halted the vast majority of the orders on a brief basis.

One test was made contrary to the FDA's standard on the circulation of mifepristone (RU-486), one of the two-section drug routines to incite early terminations. Beginning around 2000, it is just accessible through wellbeing suppliers under the FDA's decision. Because of the COVID-19 pandemic, admittance to mifepristone was a worry, and the American College of Obstetricians and Gynecologists alongside different gatherings sued to have the standard loose to permit ladies to have the option to get to mifepristone at home through mail-request or retail drug stores. While the Fourth Circuit gave a starter directive against the FDA's decision that would have permitted more extensive conveyance, the Supreme Court requested in a 6-3 choice in January 2021 to put a stay on the order, keeping up with the FDA's rule.

Chapter 4

Metropolitan safe-haven for the unborn

Starting around 2019, the counter fetus removal development in the United States has been pushing for hostile to early termination rules, for example, statements of "metropolitan safe-haven for the unborn". In June 2019, the city board of Waskom, Texas, cast a ballot to ban early termination in the city, pronouncing Waskom a "metropolitan safe-haven for the unborn" (the principal such city to assign itself in that capacity), as state legislatures somewhere else in the United States likewise were drafting fetus removal bans. As of June-July 2019, there is no early termination center in the city. The Waskom statute has driven other little urban communities in Texas, and as of April 2021 in Nebraska, to cast a ballot for becoming "metropolitan safe-havens for the unborn".

On April 6, 2021, Hayes Center, Nebraska, turned into the principal city in Nebraska to prohibit fetus removal by nearby mandate, proclaiming itself a "metropolitan safe-haven for the unborn." The city of Blue Hill, Nebraska, followed after accordingly and ordered a comparable statute banning early termination on April 13, 2021. In May 2021, Lubbock, Texas, with a populace of under 270,000, cast a ballot to turn into the biggest city in the U.S. to boycott fetus removal with the "metropolitan safe-haven for the unborn ordinance".

Abortion funding

The fetus removal banter has likewise been stretched out to the subject of who pays the clinical expenses of the methodology, for certain states involving the component as an approach to lessening the number of abortions.[citation needed] The expense of early termination shifts relies upon elements like area, office, timing, and kind of system. In 2005, a non-emergency clinic fetus removal at 10 weeks' development went from

$90 to $1,800 (normal: $430), though an early termination at 20 weeks' growth went from $350 to $4,520 (normal: $1,260).[citation needed] Costs are higher for a clinical fetus removal than a first-trimester careful abortion.[citation needed] different assets from help associations are accessible to add to the expenses of the system, as well as movement expenses.

Abortion store associations

Various associations offer monetary help for individuals looking for fetus removals, including travel and other expenses. Access Reproductive Care-Southeast (ARC Southeast), the Brigid Alliance, the Midwest Access Coalition (MAC), and the National Network of Abortion Funds are instances of such groups.

Medicaid

The Hyde Amendment is a government regulative arrangement notwithstanding the utilization of bureaucratic Medicaid assets to pay for early terminations with the exception of assault and incest. The arrangement, in different structures, was because of Roe v. Swim, and has been regularly connected to yearly appointments bills starting around 1976, and addressed the main major official accomplishment by the supportive of life development. The law expects that states cover early terminations under Medicaid in case of assault, interbreeding, and life danger. In view of the government regulation, 32 states, and D.C. store early terminations through Medicaid just in the instances of assault, interbreeding, or life peril. SD covers fetus removals just in the instances of life risk, which doesn't conform to government necessities under the Hyde Amendment. IN, UT, and WI have extended inclusion to ladies whose actual wellbeing is risked, and IA, MS, UT, and VA likewise incorporate fetal anomaly cases.

17 states (AK, AZ, CA, CT, HI, IL, MD, MA, MN, MT, NJ, NM, NY, OR, VT, WA, WV) utilize their own assets to cover all or most "therapeutically fundamental" fetus removals looked for by low-pay ladies under Medicaid, 12 of which are expected by State court requests to do so.

Confidential protection 5 states (ID, KY, MO, ND, OK) confine protection inclusion of fetus removal administrations in confidential plans: OK restricts inclusion to life risk, assault, or interbreeding conditions; and the other four states limit inclusion to instances of life peril.

11 states (CO, KY, MA, MS, NE, ND, OH, PA, RI, SC, VA) limit fetus removal inclusion in protection plans for public representatives, with CO and KY confining protection inclusion of early termination for any reason.

U.S. regulations additionally boycott government subsidizing of fetus removals for administrative representatives and their wards, Native Americans covered by the Indian Health Service, military staff and their wards, and ladies with handicaps covered by Medicare.

Mexico City strategy

Principal article: Mexico City strategy

Under this strategy, U.S. government financing to NGOs that give early termination isn't allowed. The strategy was first reported by President Ronald Reagan in 1984. It has been repealed by Democratic presidents and reestablished by Republican presidents. The strategy was revoked in 2021 by President Joe Biden.

Clinical early terminations

A Guttmacher Institute study of fetus removal suppliers assessed that early clinical fetus removals represented 17% of all non-emergency clinic fetus removals and somewhat north of one-fourth of fetus removals before 9 weeks of growth in the United States in 2008. Medical fetus removals willfully answered to the CDC by 34 detailing regions (barring Alabama, California, Connecticut, Delaware, Florida, Hawaii, Illinois, Louisiana, Maryland, Massachusetts, Nebraska, Nevada, New Hampshire, Pennsylvania, Tennessee, Vermont, Wisconsin, and Wyoming) and distributed in its yearly early termination reconnaissance reports have expanded consistently since the September 28, 2000, FDA endorsement of mifepristone (RU-486): 1.0% in 2000, 2.9% in 2001, 5.2% in 2002, 7.9% in 2003, 9.3% in 2004, 9.9% in 2005, 10.6% in 2006, 13.1% in 2007, 15.8% in 2008, 17.1% in 2009 (25.2% of those at under 9 weeks gestation). Medical early terminations represented 32% of first-trimester early terminations at Planned Parenthood facilities in 2008. By 2020, drug early terminations represented over half of all abortions.

Chapter 5

Early termination and religion

A greater part of fetus removals are gotten by strictly distinguished ladies. As per the Guttmacher Institute, "in excess of 7 of every 10 U.S. ladies getting a fetus removal report a strict connection (37% protestant, 28% Catholic, and 7% other), and 25% go to strict administrations no less than one time each month. The fetus removal rate for protestant ladies is 15 for every 1,000 ladies, while Catholic ladies have a marginally higher rate, 20 for every 1,000."

Did you know?
Pregnant individuals with solid strict religious views on abortion are in a similar extent as all individuals. As a matter of fact, most religions support the right and obligation of individuals to pursue their own pregnancy choices. Around here at Northland Family Planning Centers, we regard your strict convictions and your otherworldliness, and we comprehend that your confidence means a lot to you.

Certain individuals have a tangled outlook on their pregnancy decision, particularly the decision of fetus removal, and their strict lessons. This is entirely typical. What you will find, as you investigate your qualities, feelings, and sentiments, is that the choice of when to become a mother is an extremely private one. The capacity to settle on moral choices - like the choice about whether to proceed with a pregnancy - is the premise of a singular's nobility and independence. Maybe the accompanying words and wellsprings of data will help you. As usual, our guiding staff is prepared to tune in and assist you with finding the devices you want to pursue the choice that is ideal for you. We can allude you to the support of decision ministry, sites, or readings that will give data about religion and fetus removal.

We urge you to look somewhat more profound into your religion. You might find surprisingly resistance.

Early termination can be an extremely upright choice
Numerous choices in our lives are ethically or profoundly tested. We settle on insightful choices in view of what we are familiar with ourselves, our circumstances, and what we bring to the table. Not all choices are blissful, however, we have the solidarity to request help and direction and afterward settle on a choice that isn't hands down the best, yet one we can feel content with now and tomorrow.

In the midst of moral choices like this, a significant number of us go to our congregation or our religion for direction, support, and once in a while, pardoning. Once in a while, we find all we want in the open arms of our congregation - and in some cases not. Assuming you are concerned that the decision of early termination may not be acknowledged by your congregation or religion, if it's not too much trouble, read on or visit a portion of the supportive connections recorded here. You have the power to consider this choice insightfully, to pursue an ethical decision, and realize that you have done the best for your life and those you care about.

The acknowledgment of ourselves as great, as adored and adorable comes from inside ourselves. We are our own hardest pundit and the most troublesome individual to request absolution is our own self! Large numbers of us consider ourselves to be strict or potentially profound, but, hold ourselves to a norm of flawlessness that we wouldn't expect of any other person. An accidental pregnancy focuses a splendid light on your life - all we have been from before, what we are and what we bring to the table in our present, and everything we could ever hope for and plans for a brilliant future.

Abortions and nationality

Abortion rates will generally be higher among minority ladies in the U.S. In 2000-2001, the rates among dark and Hispanic ladies were 49 for each 1,000 and 33 for every 1,000, separately, versus 13 for each 1,000 among non-Hispanic white ladies. Note that this figure incorporates all ladies of regenerative age, including ladies that are not pregnant. As such, these fetus removal rates mirror the rate at which U.S. ladies of conceptive age have an early termination each year.

In 2004, the paces of fetus removal by nationality in the U.S. were 50 fetus removals for each 1,000 people of color, 28 early terminations for every 1,000 Hispanic ladies, and 11 early terminations for each 1,000 white women.

Chapter 6

In-state versus out-of-state - at the season of Roe v. Swim

Roe v. Swim sanctioned early termination cross country in 1973. In 1972, 41% of early terminations were performed on ladies outside their condition of home, while in 1973 it declined to 21%, and afterward to 11% in 1974.

A 1998 study revealed that in 1987 to 1988, women reported the following as their primary reasons for choosing an abortion:

Percentage of women	Primary reason for choosing an abortion
25.5%	Want to postpone childbearing
21.3%	Cannot afford a baby
14.1%	Has relationship problem or partner does not want pregnancy
12.2%	Too young; parent(s) or other(s) object to pregnancy
10.8%	Having a child will disrupt education or employment

7.9%	Want no (more) children
3.3%	Risk to fetal health
2.8%	Risk to maternal health
2.1%	Other

The source of this information takes findings into account from 27 nations including the United States, and therefore, these findings may not be typical for any one nation.

According to a 1987 study that included specific data about late abortions (i.e., abortions "at 16 or more weeks' gestation"), women reported that various reasons contributed to their having a late abortion:

Percentage of women	Reasons contributing to a late abortion
71%	Woman did not recognize she was pregnant or misjudged gestation
48%	Woman had found it hard to make arrangements for an earlier abortion
33%	Woman was afraid to tell her partner or parents

24%	Woman took time to decide to have an abortion
8%	Woman waited for her relationship to change
8%	Someone had earlier pressured woman not to have an abortion
6%	Something changed sometime after the woman became pregnant
6%	Woman did not know timing is important
5%	Woman did not know she could get an abortion
2%	A fetal problem was diagnosed late in pregnancy
11%	Other

In 2000, cases of rape or incest accounted for 1% of abortions.

A 2004 study by the Guttmacher Institute reported that women listed the following amongst their reasons for choosing to have an abortion:

Percentage of women	Reason for choosing to have an abortion
74%	Having a baby would dramatically change my life
73%	Cannot afford a baby now
48%	Do not want to be a single mother or having relationship problems
38%	Have completed my childbearing
32%	Not ready for another child
25%	Do not want people to know I had sex or got pregnant
22%	Do not feel mature enough to raise a(nother) child
14%	Husband or partner wants me to have an abortion
13%	Possible problems affecting the health of the fetus

12%	Concerns about my health
6%	Parents want me to have an abortion
1%	Was a victim of rape
less than .5%	Became pregnant as a result of incest

A 2008 National survey of family growth(NSFG) shows that rates of unintended pregnancy are highest among Blacks, Hispanics, and women with lower socio-economic status.

- 70% of all pregnancies among Black women were unintended
- 57% of all pregnancies among Hispanic women were unintended
- 42% of all pregnancies among White women were unintended

www.ingramcontent.com/pod-product-compliance
Lightning Source LLC
Chambersburg PA
CBHW080438220526
45465CB00009B/3335